SKIRTING

SKIRTING
Your "Who" Is Overdue!

Dr. Belinda J. Bell

XULON PRESS

Xulon Press
2301 Lucien Way #415
Maitland, FL 32751
407.339.4217
www.xulonpress.com

© 2022 by Dr. Belinda J. Bell

Contribution by: Janice English, EdD and Phillip Tate

All rights reserved solely by the author. The author guarantees all contents are original and do not infringe upon the legal rights of any other person or work. No part of this book may be reproduced in any form without the permission of the author.

Due to the changing nature of the Internet, if there are any web addresses, links, or URLs included in this manuscript, these may have been altered and may no longer be accessible. The views and opinions shared in this book belong solely to the author and do not necessarily reflect those of the publisher. The publisher therefore disclaims responsibility for the views or opinions expressed within the work.

Unless otherwise indicated, Scripture quotations taken from the King James Version (KJV) – *public domain.*

Scripture quotations taken from the Amplified Bible (AMP). Copyright © 1954, 1958, 1962, 1964, 1965, 1987 by The Lockman Foundation. Used by permission. All rights reserved.

Scripture quotations taken from the English Standard Version (ESV). Copyright © 2001 by Crossway, a publishing ministry of Good News Publishers. Used by permission. All rights reserved.

Scripture quotations taken from The Message (MSG). Copyright © 1993, 1994, 1995, 1996, 2000, 2001, 2002. Used by permission of NavPress Publishing Group. Used by permission. All rights reserved.

Paperback ISBN-13: 978-1-66286-050-8
Ebook ISBN-13: 978-1-66286-051-5

Dedication

I am honored to dedicate this book to my husband, Dr. Charles Bell, a man full of the Holy Spirit and my greatest cheerleader who believed in me before I could believe in myself. I also dedicate this book to all those on life's journey to discover God's purpose for their lives.

Acknowledgement

I want to thank my Lord and Savior Jesus Christ for the love, courage, and strength that supported me throughout the process of writing Skirting. My husband Charles deserves my special thanks for allowing the Lord's wisdom, guidance, patience, and love to assist and support me through the journey. I acknowledge my mom, Mrs. Nita Nance, as being courageous and wise. Dr. Janice English as editor and one of the greatest people I have met. She provided strength and encouragement and helped me find my footing throughout the book's completion. I acknowledge our children, Lori, Victoria, Elizabeth, and Katherine.

I also acknowledge Mrs. Cortese Hunt, who departed this life prior to completing this book for the delightful conversations during some of my most difficult times. I also recognize my brothers, Arnold, Phillip, Timothy, and Martin. I offer special thanks for my brother Phillip for sharing his gift of artwork throughout the book. Finally, remembering, reflecting, and writing were not the only challenges I faced, but the process of living and self-discovery were the ones I had to learn to embrace.

Foreword

***Skirting* Foreword**

Consulting with Dr. Belinda Bell on her life-changing book *Skirting* is at the top of my list of professional joys. The authenticity of her voice drew me in and so many of her insights resonated with me as I know they will with others. Whether in my role as an executive vice president, workforce development consultant, career counselor, or even currently, as a college professor, teaching at a local community college, navigating several careers has provided me with a unique perspective on Dr. Bell's powerful narrative. Rarely does a story resonate with me so fully, because Dr. Bell's book is full of personal and spiritual wisdom woven seamlessly together. Reading her words inspired me and reminded me: our purpose is to be our brother's keeper. In telling her story so clearly and compellingly, the book will provide insights focused on how we can design a life that allows us to be of benefit to others. Each of us who has a tale this powerful, a true firsthand account of how to overcome adversity, each voice should share it. This is precisely what Dr. Bell has done in providing us with her emotional testimony in *Skirting*.

Dr. Belinda Bell entered my life when she married my cousin, Dr. Charles Bell, MD, in 1989. To their union, they added four beautiful daughters. Quite unassuming. I immediately saw radiated talented and had a heart of gold. With so many things in common; a passion for cooking, a love of family, and a desire to help others, Dr. Bell has been a source of light in the life of those who surround her. Bravely entering into social media through various platforms, she seeks opportunities to be of use to others. You can find her on Face Book and YouTube following for "Mrs. Bell's Sweet Treat & More." Dr. Bell thrives through encouraging other, reminding all of us that cooking takes courage and provides creativity! What a wonderful resource to have in life, and we have shared many ideas and countless recipes over the years.

Beyond authoring books, Belinda is an Instagrammer; her hashtag is "Extra in Every Ordinary," where she has shared many heartfelt stories to illustrate the power of service to others. Dr. Bell states *No one is Just-a-Anything we're all extraordinary*! Her Facebook page welcomes all of us to gather close with Belinda Bell: Time with Grandma. Leveraging modern technology, Dr. Bell sought to connect to her grandchildren who are not local, so she uses Zoom and videos of crafting, cooking, and playing games with her grands. Children can log in and learn how to cook and play games. Her first published book is inspired by the birth of her girls, all born in different seasons of the year. "Oh, the Day that you were born;" a book of poems about each of her daughters being born in their unique season, at a specific time, on a particular day; Dr. Bell embraces recognizing the miracle of your baby!

In an effort to help others move from past struggles to an extraordinary and abundant life, the book: *Skirting* reveals Dr. Bell's desires and inspiration in sharing her moving story to provide a vision of how to overcome adversity. Learning how to overcome the stumbling blocks and pitfalls that life deals so many of us. As she states in the book, "I realized I can never go further than my thoughts," an eye-opening and foundational truth that many of us have not come to understand and apply to our lives. *Skirting* illustrates how powerful and polarizing our thoughts or thinking can be, making it difficult to be in full control of our lives.

Through her use of twin concepts of "Who"ing and "Do"ing allows you, as the reader, to experience her story of finding her identity. Who should read this book? I see *Skirting* as a life enhancing tool, a lifeline of hope for many individuals, whether their place in life or spiritual orientation. The book asks a series of questions: "Do you believe what's happened to you is who you are?" Dr. Bell chose to share *Skirting* from a place of her spirituality and beliefs and deeply felt Christian values. The book is beneficial to any person who is struggling with their past or present deep intergenerational traumas.

As Dr. Bell shares her harrowing trials and life-altering issues of her past openly, Her words are not just a few profound nuggets that can help lift a person from the plights of their past; her story can help individuals build a bridge to a hopeful and promising future. *Skirting* is a powerful testimony of profoundly human life struggles and the book articulates a guided pathway to move one to positive self-esteem, courageousness, inner strength, and God's excellent promises.

Dr. Janice English
Entrepreneur
& Educator

Skirting

Dr. Belinda J. Bell

Lilias Trotter: Parables of the Cross

> "Take the very hardest thing in your life the place of difficulty, outward or inward, and expect God to triumph gloriously in that very spot. Just there He can bring your soul to blossom!"

Table of Contents

Introduction xvii

1   The Woman in the Pool 1

2   Understanding the Foundation of "Do" 9

3   From "Do"ing to "Who"ing 21

4   Skirting Skirts 29

5   Discovery: Transitioning from "Do"ing to "Who"ing 36

Conclusion 49

Introduction

It was the first time I had ever heard the phrase *"skirting the edge of the pool,"* and that day had begun like every other: I had awakened to darkness, overwhelming feelings of hopelessness, fear, defeat, insecurity, and disappointment. Each night was a repeat of the last. I had gone to bed exhausted, frustrated, and filled with condemnation. Another day went by with no relief from those overwhelming feelings, all of which was compounded by the fear they would never abate. Although a Christian, I lived in a perpetual cycle marked by failure, insecurity, inferiority, and inadequacy. I cannot recall when the thoughts began. They have been there as far back as I can remember, and their familiarity has acted as a constant reminder that I accepted those feelings as my own.

Initially, I attributed these thoughts and feelings to a need to do something? Perhaps I was not grateful enough? Maybe I should spend more time in prayer? It might be that I needed to make a career change or go back to school? After all, I believed a change would occur if I was doing the right things. I believed it was up to me to figure out what I needed to do to protect myself and ultimately be free from defeat. Since I believed I had to do something I never once considered examining my thoughts nor understood that there were patterns of defeat. I seemed trapped in repeating negative patterns in various areas of my life, including financial, relational, and emotional. I read numerous books on making financial breakthroughs and fixing relationships. I downloaded and purchased popular series and went about doing what they said.

    I used positive affirmations and attended the latest local, national and international conferences that related to my life issues. These were the most popular "fix yourself" programs that I followed to the letter but they did not fix me. Despite short periods of relief, the patterns continued to manifest themselves. The chaos of my life, finances and relationships seemed capable of being broken down into doable pieces—if only I knew what those pieces were and what needed to be *fixed*!

    After losing our jobs, my husband and I made difficult decisions about our next steps. Just at this time, I received and accepted an invitation to visit family and welcomed the getaway. I was hoping the time away from some of the stress would provide me with a new perspective and help determine our next plan of action! In addition to being unemployed and everything this entails—

financial worries, relationship conflicts, and emotional upheavals—I was also dealing with other disappointments in my academic career and still reeling from yet another failure there. It was indeed a very challenging time. I fantasized that the getaway would be the catalyst we needed to transform our lives and stop the patterns of loss and the accompanying thoughts and feelings of despair.

The time spent visiting friends and family was exciting and most welcome. However, the feelings of dark apprehension and loss were never far away. On the final day, before I was to return home the next day, I was relaxing and reading my journal posts from the previous day. One read, *"Such a beautiful morning I get to experience... it is good God!"* I was then suddenly overcome with the losses and the thoughts and feelings that had plagued me for many years. They all seemed to join forces to harass and overwhelm me even more so than before. However, this time was different; every word I tried to formulate in my head *screamed* defeat and the end. Each word seemed to have a life of its own and my thoughts were only of regret and goodbye—as though life were about to end.

This mental assault continued until, suddenly, somewhere inside me I stood up and said, I will not go out like this! There is more to this life than what I have seen. I want what belongs to me and I will not be denied! The words did not emerge from my mind;

they sprang from my very being. Almost as quickly as the thoughts and feelings came, they were silenced and the overwhelming feelings ceased. Caught off guard, I sat down and tried to understand what had just happened. At the same time, I was reveling in and grateful for the silence.

While sitting there, I became aware of the sound of moving water interrupting and changing the trajectory of my thoughts. Although the sound of the pool water had always been there, I had never noticed it. It was not loud or intrusive. In fact, it was strangely calming and soothing, and it seemed to be drawing me to the pool. I stood up, walked across the room, and saw the pool in front of me as I opened the door. The sound of the water seemed to grow louder as I found myself standing right beside the pool.

Chapter 1

THE WOMAN IN THE POOL

Time seemed to stand still and the moment had a tangible quality. I knew the scene had been set for me; it was one of those moments when you just know to listen and pay attention—for just that moment in time. I saw the water in the middle of the pool freely moving, bobbing up and down. The up and down movement caused tiny waves that moved from one end of the pool only to crash against the opposite wall of the pool then reverse course. Dead leaves, dead bugs, and scattered debris were floating on the water. The dead things were moving and bobbing up and down with the movement of each wave. They followed the path of the waves ever so subtly, being driven up and down, back and forth, to the wall and then back into the deep.

My gaze was drawn to the side of the pool wall and there I saw the back of a woman's head and shoulders just above the water and her body outline below the surface. Although I did not immediately see her face, I observed her movements. She seemed to be stuck against the wall and tangled in dead leaves, dead bugs, and debris. The desperation with which she grabbed at the debris was evident and she never moved away from the edge of the pool. While watching her, I heard the Lord say, *"She's skirting the edge of the pool wall."* Slowly, the woman turned to look at me and I recognized the face—it was mine! It was me, skirting the edge of the pool wall?

Now, I was no longer standing there looking at the woman I was her, in the water, skirting the edge of the pool wall. There in the water, I found there was just enough room to grasp what was in front of me. I never moved beyond the wall but merely skirted along the edges while maintaining a firm grip on the pool wall. I thought, how could I go from hearing loud words screaming in my head, to this peaceful moment, and now skirting the edge of the pool? What was I doing in the water, why was I skirting and what was preventing me from moving away from the wall and into deeper water?

Then, I heard the Lord say, *"You know your do but you don't know your who?"* I repeated, I know my *"do,"* but I don't know my *"who?"* What? Of course, I know who I am! He replied, *"Then who are you?"* I thought that was a simple question. After all, I know exactly who I am; Belinda, wife, mother, Christian…I then began rattling off my accomplishments, relationships, and reputation. The Lord responded, *"No, those are not who you are! Who were you before you were born and given your name, Belinda… before you married, gave birth to children, joined a church, worked a job, before you did anything…who were you then?"*

I thought long and hard about this question and continued answering the Lord with my accomplishments, but each response from Him was the same, *"That is not who you are."* I was frustrated and finally said… everything I told you… these things *are* who I am; it is the only way I know how to be! The Lord responded, *"This is a true statement… but this is not who you are because I have always known you even before you did or knew anything?"* At that moment, I was reminded of Jeremiah 1:5; Before I formed you in the womb I knew you [and approved of you as My chosen instrument], and before you were born, I consecrated you [to Myself as My own] (AMP).

Then the Lord said, *"You do not know who you are; you only know what you have done, what's happened to you, and your accomplishments and failures. Because of your past, you began believing in your ability to protect yourself. As a result, you began making decisions to carry out your do that did not align with who you are. The alignment of your do to your past kept you in a perpetual cycle of doing; much like skirting the edge of the pool wall gathering dead things, and losing your who identity."*

The Lord gave me to understand that I skirted the edge of the pool wall, which was my reality, my truth, gathering through *"do"*ing as many trophies as I could.

Those trophies—dead bugs, dead leaves, and debris—were my old way of "do"'ing; my accomplishments, the value I assigned myself that I believed would make me valuable. I hoped that by "do"ing I would eventually silence the voices of despair, fix the broken places, and transform my life. I was hoping there was something I could "do" that would lead me to find the secret formula that eluded me my entire life. But there is no formula; the answer can only be found in finding out "who" I was. And yet, I continued to trust in my ability to "do" something to fix my life.

The Lord spoke again: *"The dead things and debris in your hands… were who you hoped you could be and allowed them to define you, believing these trophies would transform you. But they are dead; they are the residue of all the things you have done while believing that your accomplishments and failures were your identities, that they encompass who you are. Who you are does not come from anything you do; it comes from your identity."* Then I heard this question; if who you are is what you do, then who are you when you can no longer "do?"

As I clung to the pool wall with one hand and the debris with the other, I was astounded; trying to understand what I was hearing…. *"You know your do, but you don't know your who…?"* At that moment, I saw myself skirting the edge of the pool wall, "do"ing just enough to look like I was moving, but not enough to venture beyond the confines of the wall. Slowly I began to see clearly; the dead leaves, bugs, and debris were not entangling me. It was me gathering each piece as though it were a trophy. My hands were full of these dead things. I noticed that the only time I ever moved beyond the wall was to strive to grab debris that lay slightly out of reach. Once I retrieved the debris, I immediately returned to the wall, skirting the edge of the pool wall again.

I realized at that moment that the wall was my safe place, the anchor I believed protected me, but I could never move beyond that "safe place."

    The Lord revealed to me that in my supposedly "safe place," I could only relive my past experiences. The "do"ing of my past caused me to continue capturing more "do"ing, to escape the past and hopefully change my future. The negative feelings became the security blanket I used to gather more trophies, and they were the lens I saw through.

Each trophy represented something done in my strength. The trophies were the "do" I believed would help me escape the dark apprehension, disappointments, and fears that had plagued me all my life. The voice of the Lord continued: *"The leaves represented where you came from, the bugs, your abilities, and the debris, the culmination of experiences. All these dead things were the skirted life you lived."* And then the Lord said:

> *"Now is the time to stop looking at the surface of your life and past and see what is happening inside you. You keep gathering ideas and quick fixes, only to find yourself in worse shape than before. The only one that can tell you who you are is the One who created you. Take my hand, and I will show you who you are. Let go; move off of the wall; let go of the debris and come launch out into the deep with me!"*

But, I thought, "I cannot let go…if I am not my "do," then who am I? All I know are my trophies—and how can I let *them* go? They *are* my "who;" I'm nothing without them!" Suddenly, I was filled with fear, and I desperately held onto the wall and debris as though holding on for dear life. I held fast for a long time; then the Lord spoke quietly to me: *"You cannot follow me while at the same time staying skirted to the wall clutching those dead things; you will have to let something go."*

I was terrified… I did not know "who" I was without "do"ing, and if I was not my "do" then "who" was I? After trying all I knew to "do," I realized the only one that knew me was the one that created me.

Even though I was afraid and often did not believe I was enough, I realized there was no other place I could go but to God. I had already exhausted all my energy, resources, and time doing my "do." So I reluctantly let go of the edge of the pool wall, the dead things, and I took His outstretched hand. Immediately, I watched as the dead things floated behind me as I moved toward the deep. I felt fear and excitement all at once as His presence hovered over me. Then suddenly, I sank below the surface of the deep.

    Soon I was no longer sinking but felt like I was flying through the water! There was no fear now; only joy, peace, and anticipation… There was so much to see. I tried taking in everything! The farther He took me into the water, the clearer the waters became. I could not have known what was beneath the water. I was no longer focused on the dilemma of "do" and "who" as I was caught up in knowing God was holding my hand. I could see everything in front of me so clearly and hear sounds; I was mesmerized as He moved me effortlessly around creatures, objects, and debris.

Chapter 2

UNDERSTANDING THE FOUNDATION OF "DO"

Holding His hand, I thought back to my skirting the edge of the pool wall and remembered thinking of the potential dangers that awaited me in the deep; yet strangely enough, I saw no dangers. I could tell we were moving quickly because objects quickly appeared and disappeared before us. Then the Lord slowed down, and I could read the sign it read: "Understanding the Foundation of Do." The Lord said, *"To find out who you are, you have to begin where you are and go back to your beginning."*

I'm confused…so I asked the Lord, why did we to stop here… what does this sign mean and how will this place help me discover my "who?" The Lord replied, *"This is a look at your early days and what led you to believe your do is your who.* I stood there reading the sign as the scene before me became one I painfully recognized and I was taken back in time.

It was late afternoon in this long-forgotten place. I was about five years old and was standing in a room with mama as she hurriedly stuffed clothing into a carry box (I now know it was a suitcase). She was so focused on what she was doing that she did not pay attention to me or know I was even in the room. She did not speak a word but only looked around the room in searching for something. But what? I had no idea. Suddenly she stopped as though she had finished her search, and for the first time she acknowledged me, hastily grabbed my hand and half dragged me after her out of the house.

    Mama was walking so fast and I half-ran trying to keep up with her. I did not know where we were going; I only knew she was in a hurry. We crossed several vacant lots and abandoned buildings. Each lot was filled with debris; old bricks, broken glass, and tall weeds that cut my legs as we scurried across the lots. I was getting tired, but mama did not slow down, so I did my best to keep up with her.

Understanding the Foundation of "Do"

I thought this was strange, as she had never done this before, and I had no idea where we were going. When we finally reached a building, she slowed down stopped at the door, and knocked, and a woman opened it. Mama and the woman seemed to know each other, but the woman was a stranger to me. She walked us into her kitchen and there I saw three young boys quietly playing with wooden trains on the floor. Mama let go of my hand and set the carry case down on the kitchen floor as she and the woman began talking quietly but intensely, as though sharing a secret.

I had no idea the reason for the visit, who the woman was, or why I was there. I wondered about the woman, but mama never said anything to me so I kept quiet. Instead, I looked around the small kitchen with a counter, table and chairs in the middle of the room. Growing tired, I did not know what to do, so I sat down on one of the chairs. There was nothing on the counter except a box of Lorna Doone cookies.

Mama and the woman spoke very quickly, but I still could not determine what was being said, although I knew they were both upset. I dared not say anything, so I sat there and watched the boys playing. The boys seemed to be more interested in their trains than in me. My gaze returned to mama and the woman…I felt something was wrong but I did not know what. After what seemed like a long time, mama turned from the woman and hurriedly left the room, then the house, as I heard the door close after her. Mama did not look at me; or say a word to me, not even goodbye.

I remember that moment today as I revisit *Understanding the Foundation of Do* and the feelings came flooding back. I felt I was no longer in the kitchen, as though I was now invisible and being swallowed up by something I could not explain. I do not know how I knew, but I knew that mama was never coming back and for a long time, I just sat there quietly trying to be invisible, thinking, this cannot be happening, so if I just keep still, everything will go back to normal. But no matter how still I was, nothing ever was normal for me again.

The woman did not speak for a long time. I was confused, but I also knew I was alone, abandoned, and left in the home of what I thought was a stranger. It was only later that I discovered the woman was my mother, the boys were my younger brothers, and the woman I called 'mama' was my grandmother. Strange feelings seemed to engulf me. I was confused and wondered why mama had left without looking at me or speaking to me, and what I must have done to make her leave me.

I remember sitting quiet and still for a long time. Finally, I calmly watched the woman but did not know what to say or do, so I continued watching her as she picked up the carry box and guided me to another room. I wanted to know what to do to go back home. I waited for some miracle to fix what I was experiencing, but there was no miracle, and there was never any explanation. I moved into this new life, trying to explain my confusion as best I could by normalizing what had happened. If I am good, everything would be OK, and mama will return. If I am perfect! Other feelings were so palpable that I remember feeling more than knowing feelings of betrayal, abandonment, rejection, and the loss of belongingness. As I remember this time someone once wrote, *"You were born in the middle of a story whose beginning and ending you do not know."*

I remember thinking I must have done something bad to be here. I could not figure out what it was, but I knew it must have been awful. Reliving this scene, I feel the loss of connection and those long-ago emotions even now. This memory has been with me all my life; however, without corroboration or an explanation, it was a mere haunting recurring memory without any connection—*or so I thought*. As I remember those painful days, I lacked the mental tools to define what I was experiencing; I could only live through the experience. I also did not understand the control each had over my life.

I stood rereading the *"Understanding the Foundation of Do"* sign for a while, remembering the day I decided, in my youth, to "do" whatever I could to never let this happen again. I strived to be perfect and to find ways of "do"ing that would make me so valuable that I would never again be betrayed, abandoned, or rejected. Eventually, I would figure out what to "do" to make myself so valuable that no one would ever leave me again. I believed that all I had to "do" was to learn, "do" enough, follow the rules, and I would never again experience that pain.

I watched my younger self looking as though I were OK, but there was so much going on in my little mind then. I saw the fear in my eyes that was unseen by others, the fear that dominated my life. I did not feel safe anywhere. In addition to the difficulties of that time was molestation by family members, a secret known by those who were supposed to protect me—but did not. These experiences left me feeling even more betrayed, abandoned, and rejected.

Time passed and I grew older. I remember never being able to truly trust anyone. At the same time, I never felt I was enough. I believed that whatever good things happened to me would be because of something I did and that the feelings would disappear once I did enough of that thing. I believed that "do"ing would provide explanations, protection, and value. I seriously believed I had to "do" more, be more, and work harder than anyone else to make up for what I thought I was *not*.

Working My "Do"

We moved from the house to my early days of working. I was excited then and thus failed to recognize "do"ing patterns. I only welcomed the "do"ing to demonstrate my value. There were times when working and "do"ing kept the negative feelings at bay, but it was always for a short period, as though the "do"ing interrupted the negative feelings; or so it seemed. So, I thought, all I have to do is "do" more and once I did more or enough or the right combination of "do"ing, the negative feelings and repeated negative patterns would cease, but they did not. In spite of that, I continued "do"ing throughout my teens and into adulthood. I became consumed with taking on tasks and assignments no one else wanted.

What is "Do?"

For anything to be accomplished requires the act of doing. "Do"ing is neither good nor bad, but it does require a reason or motivation; I *did this because of that!* My "do" was motivated by events that drove me to making decisions to act following a fearful or traumatic event. Following this idea, my "do" focused on a specific issue requiring change, correction, or removal. My "do" was also motivated by circumstances requiring change and will necessitate more "do"ing when something new occurs. For example, when mama abandoned me, I decided I must "do" something to become so valuable no one would abandon me again. My value was rooted in what I could "do." What I failed to understand, then, was that my "do" adapted to each event, producing another "do" strategy with little success. I figured out what to "do" with each event and applied what I figured out until another event arose.

It became apparent to me that the "do"ing motivated by "who"ing was different from what I previously stated was my reason for "do"ing. My "do"ing was rooted in what was done to me or what I had done. Therefore the foundation of my "do" was not rooted in who I am in Christ and the blood He shed for me. Consequently, my previous "do" did not have an identity. But "do"ing attached to "who" I am is rooted in Christ. I love others and myself because of who I am in Christ. Without Christ, my "do" was rooted in my own abilities, efforts, and experiences that continue to shift as circumstances change. My "do" without "who" believed that gathering trophies would fix the negative patterns of my life. I also recognized that my "do" was always a future action; I will do this tomorrow, the next time or when I get where I am going…

Looking back at my younger self, I recognized the perpetual feeling of waiting for the other shoe to drop. I remember hearing and quickly accepting Jesus Christ as my personal Savior by age nineteen. I recalled the peace that followed my decision as I began a new relationship and embraced this new phase in my life. I was so excited; I wanted everyone to know about Jesus Christ! I believed I had to follow doctrinal and behavioral guidelines to be loved by God. However, it would take many years before I realized that salvation was not about rules and traditions but rather about the love of God for me in sending His Son, Jesus Christ, to die in my place.

I missed this point as I strived to do my "do," believing that the work Jesus Christ did on the cross and His rising from the dead required me to do my part, so that with Jesus Christ, we could "do" more together! I erroneously did my "do" based on my fear that if I did not "do," I would have no value and that my "do" was surely the only reason God could love me. At the time I failed to realize, that the plan of salvation was about relationships, not a list of dos and don'ts. I spent years searching for what to "do," following what someone said I should "do," or "do"ing what I thought I was supposed to "do."

I believed the lie that the "do"ing would lead me to stumble onto my purpose. I also believed that this purpose stemmed from what I was good at and that all I had to do was keep "do"ing and eventually find it. However, I failed to realize the why of doing;

that my "do"ing was often prompted by fear and by changes I could not control, generating ongoing confusion, feelings of abandonment, and rejection. Reliving this time in my life, I was again reminded that I was skirting the edge of the pool wall and feeling the constant awareness that I was not enough.

"Do"ing was not always negative as it often resulted in exciting times to learn new skills and abilities. However, I began to see "do"ing as a temporary distraction from the feelings and disappointments that beset me. I believed all my hopes and dreams were wrapped in my ability to "do" and I always aspired to "do" more. In the end, "do"ing led to more doing, and eventually, I wondered when I would finally arrive at the place where I would be enough and the voices would stop.

Facing the possibility that "do"ing may not be enough, I became fearful that no matter how much I did, I could never "do" enough, and so I hopelessly resigned to the belief I would never *be* enough! I also felt that "do"ing would never make the negative feelings disappear. Moreover, I began to accept there was always far more "do"ing that needed to be done—and that it was impossible for me to do it all! But "do"ing was all I had, *right?*

My need to "do" led to patterns of "do"ing to exhaustion, confusion, seasons of condemnation and regret and the overwhelming belief that I was not enough. I never considered focusing on myself to find out what was going on with me, because that would take time away from "do"ing. If I did that, I might miss the magic moment when everything would make sense; after all, my "do" held my attention as I struggled with acceptance.

Since I saw myself as my "do," I did not realize there were things hidden in my past that I knew nothing about. A constant voice was crying out to me during these times—but I chose to ignore it as a distraction from "do"ing. After all, I thought, who would truly love me if they really knew me? I relentlessly adhered to church doctrines; I volunteered and incorporated my "do" into every area of my life. I attended every church function, followed the rules of dress and behavior, and quickly embraced the role of church doer. I gave willingly, devoting time and energy to church activities, performing tasks and making myself available whenever needed. Yet despite this flurry of "do"ing, there remained a void.

Although I sang "Yes Jesus Loves Me" on Sunday with all the gusto I could muster, my thoughts constantly conflicted with what the Bible said I was and who I thought I was. I did my "do" to make myself worthy because I could not possibly be worthy of God's love. So I did my "do" to be worthy; praying, fasting, attending seminars, reading yet more books—and the patterns still continued. I became so focused on "do"ing that even relationships became a list of do's and don'ts. For a long time, I decided that there must be something wrong with me and that if I kept working on "do"ing, I would be able to figure out what that thing was.

Please understand me; there were wonderful times in my life when I saw my prayers answered, which included being protected amid difficult and odd situations; miraculous healings, opened financial doors, and wisdom in the circumstances beyond my control. One of the greatest blessings was when the Lord sent my husband Charles; we married and raised four beautiful and intelligent daughters together. For a while, I felt I had found the answer to the dark apprehensive thoughts; all I had to "do" was stay busy, meaning "do" more!

Being a wife and mother, working, volunteering, and returning to college dominated my time and thoughts for many years. However, the earlier feelings were never far away. While there were times I thought I had finally found the solution, they were short-lived. I falsely attributed the results to "do"ing tasks in a particular way. I followed this process for many years, working feverishly, and filling myself with more "do."

I continued "do"ing more or finding new ways to "do" more to rid me of the feelings and escape defeat. For many years I did my "do" and I felt like the donkey chasing the carrot attached to her head for most of those years. But instead of stopping, I figured I just needed to "do" more and that things would suddenly change.

Eventually, I believed that victory would never be mine after much "do"ing and yet without long-standing results. Moreover, the negative feelings increased, bringing new ones; insecurity, inferiority, loneliness, and depression. I began to believe that these feelings and repeated patterns were my crosses to bear for the rest of my days.

One day I was in the kitchen going over something else I had to "do" in my head when I remembered a line from the movie *The Wizard of Oz*. Dorothy and her friends were almost at the end of their journey and about to receive what they longed for. Each of her friends received an answer from the wizard's black bag; however, Dorothy longed to return home and said to the Wizard, "I don't think there's anything in that black bag for me." I remember that those words spoke to the void within me—and I recognized there just was not another "do" I could "do;" maybe I was beyond God's help and I was looking for what I needed in the wrong place.

I heard myself say, I already did the "do"s and followed every instruction to the letter. I made declarations and decrees, shouted positive affirmations, and committed to memory the next "fix-it program." All of this, hoping that "do"ing all of this would finally flick that elusive, magical switch that would miraculously catapult me into freedom and victory in those areas I constantly struggled with… that elusive place where God would finally answer me. But here I was again doing my "do"—and again, my "do" did not work!

I prayed to escape from the giants in my life only to find myself in the same cycle of unanswered prayers, facing an even bigger version of "Goliath." I felt more than heard that it was time to move on, yet I had so many unanswered questions. I was always full of "do"ing. I asked, so was "do"ing wrong and why was "do"ing not enough? And if it's not enough, then who am I without my "do?"

Chapter 3

From "Do"ing to "Who"ing

I searched for an answer yet again, and this time I did not try to figure it out but instead went straight to the source. There I stood, tired and frustrated, and I did not utter words I believed were spiritual or use the ideas introduced in my last trend. I simply asked, "God who am I?" His response was immediate!

> *"You are asking who you are… this is good… Let me first tell you who I am. I am the one that made you in my image and likeness, not according to your failures! You were never an afterthought. I am the one that loves you always. I am the One who created you with purpose, on purpose, for purpose and My rule is not limited to your circumstances. You are my daughter, the daughter of the Most High God! I have always known you, even when you did not trust me, when you ignored me. When you accepted Jesus Christ as your Savior you are my daughter; an heir of God, and joint heir with Christ "(Romans 8:16-17 KJV).*

But I do not understand; if I am who you say I am, an heir of God, then why is my life such a mess? If I am all these things to you, then why am I struggling in every area of my life with the same issues year after year? Why is my life a perpetual list of do's and don'ts without victory? The next words cut me to my core:

> "Because you do not know who you are. It has always been true but you did not believe me. The experiences of your past—betrayal, abandonment, and rejection—invade your thoughts and thus influence your life. These experiences have voices saying, of course, you are not enough, but if you do this or that, then you will be enough."

As I listened to His words it was not difficult to understand why I felt defeated. My "do"ing was attached to circumstances, so my "do"ing changed when those circumstances changed. My "do"ing was entrenched in my efforts what I could do…rather than what has already been done for me. But God made me to know my "who" is different. "Who" I am does not change based on circumstances; it is who I am in spite of them. "Who" I am is my identity.

Identity Crisis

I became aware that the pattern of "do"ing always ended in defeat because what you do is not who you are thus, the patterns would begin again; "do," then defeat! As previously mentioned, "do"ing was attached to circumstances, but "who" does not change based on circumstances; "who" is your identity despite circumstances. Instead of recognizing what Jesus Christ had done for me, I saw what I could "do" based on my efforts.

God helped me realize I attributed who I am to what I had done but, that He alone had made me to be who I am. I began to understand that my "do"ing was often generated by an event that compelled me to figure out what I needed to do to protect myself or prevent further harm. I also described "do"ing in terms of roles or titles, beliefs, and others' opinions, believing I was what I was supposed to "do."

As I tried to absorb all of this, the Lord began to speak on my "who:" *"Your who comes from the identity I gave you and was present before you were ever born. Your who is not at the mercy of what has happened to you, what you have been through or even what you think or believe. Your who identity is not found in your past, mess-ups, sins, or mistakes. It is not found in the good or bad things you have done or done to you. Your who does not change; your who is who you are despite what has happened to you. Your who stands on its own, even when others do not agree or like it. But you allowed your do to define who you are."*

Finally, I realized "do"ing was the only way I knew how to be. As a result, I attached a plan to "do" something when difficult situations occurred. But when I accepted Jesus Christ as Lord, the work was already done for me on the cross through the shedding of His Blood. As I slowly took in all the Lord told me, I began to understand that my "who" originates in the only One that knows me; not my parents, pastor, those I esteem, or any of those I trusted. The only One who knows my "who," is God, who created me.

He said:

> *"Only I know your true value, purpose, and identity. You are priceless! You accepted Jesus Christ as your Savior but did not make Him your Lord. Your experiences of betrayal, abandonment, and rejection colored your perception of who I am and who you are.*
>
> *Instead of walking in the newness of life as a new creation in Christ, you fell victim to the lies that you are damaged and of no value, that you are not enough;*

that you deserve what happened to you; and that if you want things to change, you must expend all your efforts for that purpose. You saw me as a severe uncaring task master that loved you only when you did everything right. You tried to please Me through your doing; being good, following rules, always looking for ways to please Me. You considered all of your efforts and doing would prevent the damaging effects… however, your efforts denied the completed work by my Son Jesus Christ on the Cross.

I began to realize that instead of walking in the promise as a new creation in "who" I am in Christ, I had fallen victim to the lies that my past rendered me damaged and therefore I had no value. In addition, I accepted the lie that I alone could change my circumstances using all my efforts for that purpose. I saw God as a severe uncaring task master that loved me only when I did everything right. I tried to please God through "do"ing; being good, and following rules. To accomplish this, I believed that all my "do"ing efforts would prevent further harm…however, my "do"ing efforts denied the completed work by His Son Jesus Christ on the Cross.

Instead of taking God's Word as the only say in the matter, I allowed the words of others and my thoughts, feelings, and failures to determine who I am. None of these were true. Those responsible for me—parents, teachers, and others—did not take care of me. No amount of "do"ing on my part could ever fix the broken patterns in my life; however, Jesus Christ is my redeemer and the redeemer of life and time!

The Lord let me know that although I did not know "who" I was nor did I have the knowledge missing from growing up, I could still sense that something was wrong. However, I mistakenly went about exploring using my "do," my strength, and the limited knowledge from others. God told me I could move away from the pool wall because all things are mine. I can now accept that I am His and have His name. He invited me to cast aside my old way of "do"ing attached to the past or a situation and embrace my identity in Him. Not by "do"ing but by being in Christ.

God's words helped me understand that fears and inadequacies drove me to hold on to my ways of "do"ing instead of embracing who I am in Him. I now know why I spent my life skirting the edge of the pool wall and not moving beyond that limited space. I erroneously placed my identity in what I did, could do, had done, and believed, ignoring the truth that my identity is in Christ. As one made in the image of God, I am more than a conqueror and can do all things through Christ, who gives me strength (Philippians 4:13 KJV). I am a powerful being! I thought I was not enough, that "do"ing was my identity. As a result, I followed old ways of "do"ing rather than living the life of freedom in Christ, the life that Christ died for. God reminded me that I was carrying a burden He already bore for me; that He had already completed the work and His burden is light (Galatians 2:9-21 MSG)

Christ's Identity

I realized the need to take a long, hard look at myself and remembered the image of the woman gathering dead treasures. I believed the image of who I was, my "who," was a result of my past that comprised feelings of worthlessness, fear, insecurity, and inferiority. Curious to learn more I researched identity crises and discovered that identity emanates from the inside out, not the outside in. I kept trying to fix the inside by "do"ing something on the outside. I tried numerous fixes that included more education, utilizing self-help, adhering to religious rituals and doctrines. Nevertheless, you cannot change yourself by "do"ing, because identity must come from the inside, from "who" you are, not what you "do." Your identity cannot be found outside yourself in the dead things you consider treasures. As a Believer, my identity can only be found in Jesus Christ.

I felt such relief as I realized I was not the culmination of the "do"s, mess-ups, sins, mistakes, failures, bad decisions, education, and abuse. I was not forsaken or neglected. No, I am loved, and purpose was given to me before I ever did anything. I acknowledged that no amount of "do"ing would ever lead me to discover "who" I am. Take a moment and ask yourself this; if who you are is what you "do," then who are you when you can no longer "do?" After so many years of "do"ing I finally realized purpose and identity were freely assigned to me at birth. In the act of love, God freely gave His Son for me.

In previous chapters, I wrote that "do"ing is attached to circumstances or something that happened or will happen to you. However, when "do" is attached to "who" you are, nothing is impossible for you. You "do" because you know who you are and your decisions are not based on circumstances but in what God wants. Who you are, your identity is in Christ, so you are able to "do" based on who you are in Him.

I encourage each of us to look closer and ask the Lord who we are. Is your "do" who you say you are? If so, what are you without it? Who are you when you lose your job? Who are you when circumstances rob you of the role you play? Do you identify yourself as someone God never meant you to be because you are "good at it?" Who you are is not based on anyone's opinion of you. Who you are is always present in the here and now, in what you're thinking, feeling, focusing on now, and in your thoughts on the now and your response to it.

Following this idea, "who"ing contains a reflection that centers on the now and how you got here. "Who"ing is taking each thought, determining if it is your thought, where the thought came from, and bringing it into alignment with His Word about who HE says you are. Who you are is conforming to who HE says you are.

Jesus Christ is an excellent example of following God's process of doing… Jesus always did those things that pleased the Father! He sought God's view on everything before he did anything. He prayed in faith, believing, what His Father said. Although Jesus was God and man, He chose not to call down angels to fight for Him but humbly surrendered His "do," to the will of God. He spent time in the Word to know God's view on the matter. "Do"ing without "who"ing is something we can "do" on autopilot. I did my "do" to fix myself or to solve a problem. But "do" was not attached to "who" I am. When my "do" is attached to "who" I am, nothing is impossible for me.

Lost in the Labels

An important note; it may be easy to identify yourself based on circumstances, others' perspectives, our actions, or status. Although you may often find these labels hurtful or comforting, it is important to note that labels are restricting; they keep you skirting the edge of the pool wall, and prevent you from ever moving beyond the wall (labels). The negative labels clearly reveal to us and others an identity allowing us to remain skirted. In this skirted view, you may feel lost and confused, without identity and ultimately without purpose. Remember, you are not a human "do"ing; you're a human *being*!

Guided by the Lord, I was again reminded I did not grow up with a sense of family. As a result, I began my journey to learn more about my parents' family, which ultimately led back to *their* parents. However, that journey was not straightforward, as the few that knew the history were either elderly or dead. I felt that because of the lack of information, searching was going to be a waste of time. God has a way of opening the next window once you climb through the one he offers you. Interestingly enough, the limited information provided a glimpse into my family's past and I found the same "Goliath" in their lives there. The answers were sparse, yes, but then He placed in my path people who knew how to search for information and then created situations in which those who did know reached out to me. Wow!

Before identifying "who" I was, I first had to determine who I was not. I was not the sum total of my mistakes; pride, sin, bad choices, etc. The answer to who you are may not be easy, but one that requires the Lord's help and deep reflection. The chaos in my life created my inability to separate my "do" with my "who," causing me to make choices that did not align with who God said I was. I needed to be willing to expand my limited perspective about who I thought I was. At that moment, I realized I might not be who I thought I was. So I sat there listening to God.

Attaching your "do"ing, even your successful endeavors, to anyone other than Jesus Christ will never banish your feelings of inferiority. Only your "who" identity is attached to Jesus Christ, the one who created you, who knows your true identity, who gave HIS life for you and who imbued righteousness into an account that had none; only HE has the legal right to transform you, to give you HIS identity… Following the "do"ing system you were born into only keeps you on the proverbial hamster wheel of doing more and more. This "do"ing system only resulted in more "do"ing. However, I can do all things when I attach my "do" to who I am in Christ Jesus. I realize that I allowed my "do" to rob me of my time, energy, talents, and identity. I also recognized I used "do"ing behaviors to fill voids in my life.

Chapter 4

SKIRTING SKIRTS

The previous chapters exposed skirting as my way of avoiding difficulty or a means of protection. Skirting was my way of making sense of the chaos in my life. This chapter will view the skirt as a garment attached and extended from the waist down. I used several examples of both natural skirts and the behavior I associated with them. I share with you the elements of my skirting ways—how I skirted—using the example of a natural skirt. This chapter does not label skirts as good or bad, but simply illustrates my skirting ways. The chapter also includes several skirt styles: A-line, flared, pleated, straight, and wrapped skirts. Using the natural skirt as an example was simply to demonstrate my *skirting ways*. The different skirt styles distinguished a natural skirt design and the "do"ing behavior.

Meaning Behind the Skirts

The skirts in this chapter represent an individual's behaviors and values. Skirts symbolize a person's struggle with their beliefs, emotions, thoughts, and actions. Skirt examples in this book illustrate types of skirts and are not associated with any gender. Regardless of the skirt style worn, none outweigh the other in value nor are more honorable than others but are simply skirts.

Dynamics of the A-line Skirt

The natural skirt

The natural A-line skirt resembles the letter "A." The physical shape of the A-line skirt conforms to the hips and widens slightly to the hem giving the appearance of a smaller waist or wider hips. The natural style of the skirt is clean and easy to wear, and the design easily conceals flaws. The skirt is also very versatile and popular for novice and experts. The A-line skirt follows the pattern outline and its design stays within its perimeters.

The Skirter A-line Skirt: Behaviors and Values

The skirter A-line skirt stays within the confines of its design. The skirter follows the rules and is prone to be a workaholic; possibly due to the unwillingness or inability to move beyond its limited boundaries. The skirter A-line skirt easily offers second-hand information they heard or read about what somebody said or did. The skirter A-line skirt has no qualms about sharing information and opinions or citing scriptures *(if they are religious)*. The skirter is often known as the jack of all trades and master of none. Although the skirter appears knowledgeable, often advising others on what *they* should do the skirter themselves have no personal experience.

The A-line skirter continuously aligns their "do" to their experiences, beliefs, and who they think they are. The skirter determines "who" they are by what they think they can "do" using titles and roles to define themselves. As a result, the A-line skirter conforms to rules of conduct, following "do" strategies that do not align with "who" they are. The A-line skirter filters everything through past experiences, what they think and believe about "who" they are.

Dynamics of the Flared Skirt

The Natural Flared Skirt

A natural flared skirt is made with extra fabric that fastens at the waist providing ample room for movement. The skirt fits snugly at the waist and flares toward the hem. The additional fabric in the natural flared skirt may enhance curves or offer the appearance of curves even when none are present. In addition, the flared skirt can hide flaws, bulges, and weight that tighter skirts cannot. If you view the flared skirt from overhead, the skirt resembles a perfect circle if the wearer spins. A flared skirt may improperly distort size, and while it hides certain bumps, it also may misrepresent size or height making one appear bigger or taller.

The Skirter Flared Skirt: Behaviors and Values

The skirter flare skirt's extra fabric represents the opinions and beliefs of others. The extra fabric may hide "do" behaviors and activities that consume the wearer's time and energy, often distracting them from realizing "who" they are. The additional material may leave them carrying more weight than with slimmer skirts. The extra weight may be due to the skirter using extra energy to "do" more. The extra fabric may appear to be 'flowing' when moving but a closer look discloses the 'flowing' is actually controlled by the behaviors and activities of "do." When the skirter spins in the flared skirt, the behavior is the skirting or "do"ing; however, once the skirter can no longer spin or "do," the skirt deflates and the skirter struggles to figure out what comes next.

Dynamics of the Natural Pleated Skirt

The Natural Pleated Skirt

The natural pleated skirt displays folds or creases that make for effortless movement and comfort while offering eye-catching patterns. The pleat is formed by folding the fabric back onto itself. This process requires additional fabric that increases the volume and allows the garment to breathe. Pleated skirts may vary with the number of pleats, either few or many. The pleated skirt has two distinct pleats; the exposed pleats require limited movement, while the hidden pleat is revealed when movement occurs.

The Skirter Pleated Skirt: Behaviors and Values

The skirter pleated skirt is formed by folding fabric back onto itself, resulting in two distinct identities; the exposed and hidden pleats. Additionally, both the exposed and hidden pleats require decisions about what to "do" to remain in position? The exposed pleat design allows for more effortless movement. The skirter wearing the pleated skirt believes the exposed pleat appears to welcome new ideas and strategies requiring more "do"ing to keep each pleat in a "fixed" position. However, the exposed pleat cannot remain fixed for very long. As a result, the skirters' exposed pleats constantly adjust to different circumstances to maintain their outward appearance. The only power the skirters' exposed pleat has is to hold back the hidden pleat, manipulating the circumstances.

The hidden pleat worn by the skirter, hides behind the exposed pleat because that is the only way it knows how to be. The hidden pleat makes decisions based on how much the exposed pleat allows. The hidden pleat welcomes restrictions to prevent any change to its shape or structure and will "do" whatever it takes to avoid being revealed. But in actuality, the hidden pleat has more power because without the hidden pleat the exposed pleat is just a skirt without structure. The matter is that the exposed pleat would not exist as a pleat without the hidden pleat.

The skirter pleated skirt may require re-pleating because the skirter does not know who they are and lacks identity. The closeness of the exposed and hidden pleats creates conflict that causes the skirter to make wrong decisions based on the crookedness in the folds of the pleats. The conflict creates back and forth reminders of the past that keep the skirter in a cycle of the same old experiences. Because of the reminders of the past the skirter pleated skirt does not understand the differences between "who" and "do." The experiences often cause the skirter to operate in "do"ing instead of "who"ing.

Dynamics of the Natural Straight Skirt

The Natural Straight Skirt

The natural straight or pencil skirt is a fashion favorite. The skirt style can give the illusion of confidence or sophistication. Because of the form-fitting design of the straight skirt it provides little room for movement. The movements in the straight skirt are controlled and limited, forcing the wearer to remain within certain boundaries or risk busting out of the skirt altogether. The natural straight skirt may require assistance to stand up or navigate certain environments; thus, the skirt sometimes requires a slit to facilitate walking. The natural straight skirt may also 'ride up' when sitting or twist around when walking.

The Skirter Straight Skirt: Behaviors and Values

The skirter straight skirt style offers a polished appearance as the skirt adheres closely to the wearer's body. Since the straight skirt design can only allow movement in one direction at a time, the skirter adheres to strict guiding principles without wavering. As the skirt design is one-directional, the skirter must be intentional and select truth based on what truth they deem has the most value. The inability to move in more than one direction requires the skirter to make "do" lists that focus on a single point of view; however, the skirters narrow focus never allows for downtime. As a result, the skirter only lives for the moment, what they feel, think, or believe, without knowing if what they "do" is aligned with who they are?

The straight fit combined with the need to keep "do"ing results in the life being sucked out of this skirter. They are critical of themselves and others who do not measure up to their straight standards. In addition, the skirter believes value is earned so they constantly follow their lists measuring themselves by their accomplishments or lack thereof. The straight skirter is unable to recognize "who" exists. The skirter never experiences freedom because of the heavyweight of "do" on their shoulders. This skirter is never happy with themselves or others.

Dynamics of the Wrap Skirt

The Natural Wrap Skirt

The wrap skirt is an accommodating pattern as it adjusts to the wearer's body. The skirt's design wraps material around the waist, held in place by fabric or fasteners that can easily be adjusted. The wrap portion of the skirt slightly overlaps to allow for movement without revealing too much. The skirt is flattering as it easily conforms to the wearer and the fasteners or ties help keep the skirt in place. The skirter wrap skirt may contain decorations to improve its appearance and easily adjusts by moving the fastener or ties. The design of the wrap skirt is considered an easy project for beginners.

The Skirter Wrap Skirt: Behaviors and Values

Just as the natural wrap skirt conforms to the individual, the skirter wrap skirt easily conforms to their beliefs, experiences, and understanding. The skirt is wrapped around the body of the wearers' beliefs while easily adjusting to behaviors and activities of "do"ing. These "do" behaviors and activities conform to both the opinions and beliefs of others and the skirter's experiences, insecurities, and inadequacies. The only limitation of the wrap skirt design is that the wearer must manage its boundaries. The skirt can wrap loosely to accommodate more "do"ing or wrap tightly to retain familiar "do" behaviors and activities. The skirter wrap skirt wearer may "wing it" or 'fake-it-till-they-make-it."

The loose-fitting wrap skirt energizes the belief that "do"ing will ultimately bring solutions. The tight-fit of the wrap skirt only recycles previous "do" behaviors in the hope that more "do"ing will eventually drive away the insecurities and inferiorities. Loosening or tightening the wrap skirt does not result in understanding who you are it only identifies "do"ing as who you *think* you are. For the wrap skirter, the skirt fasteners (beliefs and opinions) put in place to secure the wrap skirt can be manipulated. This may cause the skirt to unravel at inappropriate times under the weight of "do"ing. This may occur because they do not know who they are. The wrap skirt is not as secure as one may think as difficulties demonstrate the lack of security in this skirt.

Chapter 5

Discovery: Transitioning from "Do"ing to "Who"ing

How I transitioned - Overcoming the Lies

The journey to writing *Skirting* began when I finally recognized that the patterns of brokenness that continued to follow and overwhelm me. After expending all the energy "do"ing something to fix me, it became apparent I was facing the end of all the "do"ing I could *do*. Right at that place, I prepared to accept that there was nothing else I could do. Writing a book was not in my thoughts; I just wanted to be fixed. I never imagined the fixing I longed for was the healing, which would be found once I knew who I was. Although I knew I needed to change, I did not know *what* needed changing?

Perception

Perception is how I think about or understand people or things. My perception is the unique way of seeing something only I could see. Jesus revealed that my perception was how my mind explained and made sense of my circumstances. Past experiences shaped my perception and those experiences contained fear, insecurity, inferiority, and the need to control everything.

As such, those experiences and feelings impaired my perception, so I identified with "do"ing (in my own strength) and not with being (who I am). As stated previously, identity emanates from the inside out, not the outside. My identity, who I am, originates in God, and who I am is the complete person He created me to be. No circumstance or experience will ever change God's will for your life or mine! According to Malachi 3:6, I am the Lord I do not change; therefore you are not consumed… (ESV).

The Lord gave me to understand that my perception of the dead things and debris in my hands was trophies, what I hoped would make me valuable. I allowed the trophies to define me, believing that the gathering would silence the negative voices and fix the adverse outcomes in my life. The trophies reminded me of everything I mistakenly believed were who I am. He paused for a moment to allow me time to absorb what was about to say. Then He said, *"But who you are does not come from anything you do; it comes from your identity in Me."*

Then He made me know I had been gathering trophies and dead things all my life and skirting the edge of the pool wall, believing I would be safe by controlling the situation. I failed to understand that the edge of the pool wall was also my prison…a limited place that perpetually linked me to the past, its feelings, and a distorted perception of my value. I realized I could never go further than my thoughts. I needed to change my perception which begins with changing who I believe, what I think, what others said, and focus on what He said about me.

I do not know how long I sat there thinking over His words until He brought back to my memory another time when He and I saw two different points of view. I was driving home from a friend's house, late one night. Now, this was before GPS and cell phones. I was not far from home but somehow found I was completely lost. I struggled to find familiar signs to lead me home, but after about half an hour, I was on the back end of a military base, with only my headlights reflecting off parked jeeps, tanks, and equipment.

I cried out to God for help, never expecting Him to answer, but He did. A voice said, *"turn around,"* so I did. The voice then said, *"Make a left."* I looked left and it was darker than where I just came from, so I said that's not the way and proceeded to turn right. The voice said, *"How do you know when you don't know the way."* I stopped in the middle of that right turn and turned back to the left, followed His promptings and I was home within 10 minutes. My perception and failure to trust His voice was initially part of a pattern of mistrust and inability to distinguish His voice from mine. I did not trust that the voice would guide me the right way. I also realized my inability to know His voice and to trust Him was not because of Him, but because of my perception *of* Him.

Personal skirting

In Chapter Four, I identified skirting ways using examples of natural skirts. It became clear to me…I accepted skirting as my way to fix my life and to avoid or prevent future brokenness. I skirted believing that if I could "do" enough, God would love me, instead of accepting that He already loved me before I did anything. I skirted, trusting in the voices of others and ignoring what He already said about me. I skirted relying on the power of "do"ing instead of the finished work His Son Jesus Christ completed with His death, burial, and resurrection. I offered my "do" in exchange for what He had already done.

When He told me I was enough, I disagreed with Him and chose to believe I was not enough. I believed that He loved me based on my efforts. I skirted when I trusted in what I could "do." I failed to pray in faith, have belief, and trust in Him. I skirted when I assigned little value when He told me who I was in Him,

"A pearl of great price, the daughter of the Most High;" and chose to believe the lies from my past. I skirted when I ignored the truth and trusted in the lie that I had to earn God's love, and if I followed the rules, then maybe God would love me. I skirted when I failed to understand that Jesus had already overcome the world (John 16:33 KJV)! He said I was already more than a conqueror (Romans 8:37 KJV)! He promised in His Word that in Christ I can do all things (Philippians 4:13 KJV). He promised that the victory that overcomes the world is my faith (1 John 5:4 KJV), not my "do."

Walking in "do"ing I was fighting a spiritual battle using my natural "do." Jesus Christ gave me a fresh revelation of the love of God; not the church love, or the one I tried to earn…but the unconditional love of a Father for His own child. Since I had no father in my life, this was another obstacle for me to overcome but not without His grace. For the first time in a long time, I felt His presence and love I had never known, the True love God had for me. A love that saw me where I was and loved me still, in the middle of my mess, before and even after knowing me. With His help, I began to understand the true meaning of love by opening the eyes of my heart to see myself and others as He does. He reminded me that His love was not *because* I got it right, *when* I got it right, or even *if* I got it right, but His love for me is because God is love and I belong to Him.

The Revelation of God's Process

The process of finding my "who" was not a way to condemn or to make me feel guilty but to guide me to my identity. I often felt such a sense of regret that I had lost so much time asking why I did not know this…. In those times, He reminded me that no time with Him is ever wasted and that He alone is the redeemer of time. The "do"ing I did in my life was an attempt to fix all the messes in my life. But while I attempted to fix myself through more "do"ing, that "do"ing was attached to the fears from the past rather than rooted in who Christ is in me. His purpose for my life from the beginning has not changed. He is Alpha and Omega, the beginning and the end and His Word is settled forever. The Lord made me know *"Although the lies that life has dealt you, may appear to you to have altered my plans, I stand by my Word, when I say who you are."*

After much research, asking questions, praying, crying, and a myriad of emotions I learned more about my family. Even with little to no information, it was important to begin with what I knew about my family. I would like to say I asked for God's help when I started this process instead, I just jumped in. It was not long before I regretted that decision. After many clumsy starts, pursuing outdated or false information, it quickly became apparent that I could do nothing without God! Only after including God and welcoming His way of doing things was I able to move forward.

There were difficulties along the way, but just knowing God was with me every step of the way was comforting. As God's grace washed over me, the comfort of God allowed me to see I had not considered the sorrow that surrounded those telling the story or those who lived it. I only considered my feelings. I was able to see the pain of those other people. God taught me how to listen to His gentle promptings to draw information from a person that was unwilling, frightened, or ashamed. I learned when to listen to His instructions, to speak, pause, or shut up. Sometimes the conversations prompted the telling of stories, rumors, and even gossip. The gathering of my history necessitated an examination deciphering my preconceived notions, perceptions, and conclusions. Then there were times when, during casual conversations, the knowledge that had previously been withheld was suddenly revealed, opening the door to another piece of my history.

I do not want to leave the impression that everything was Kumbaya with me holding hands and skipping down the yellow brick road. History cannot be changed and there were some situations that I could not revisit safely. Not at all! I found beauty and horror as I listened to and read about members who have passed on. There were times I felt I needed to learn more but then there were instances I was just grateful I survived, and that was enough. Thank God! I was angry when I did not learn what I thought I should know, and I felt betrayed because it seemed no one considered me in their decisions. Then I came face to face with the reality that all I have is all I have and that was ok.

What would I have done differently if I knew "who" I was?

If I knew who I was, I would have known my value and not wasted so many years thinking I was not enough. If I knew "who" I was, I would have understood that my life reflected my thoughts, and that every idea has the potential to transform the direction of my life. I would have realized that thoughts can either paralyze or propel you and it was always up to me to choose which.

I would have known that everything began with my thoughts and recognized the significance of the thoughts that held me back. I would have listened to and paid attention to "who" God's Word says that I am, and not be focused on who I was *not*. I realize my thoughts were the currency that I paid for in time and effort throughout my life. If I had known then what I know now, I would not have allowed feelings of powerlessness to keep me skirted to the pool wall. No, I would have launched out into the deep and provided strategies and encouragement for others to do the same.

I would have been walking in who I was and encouraging others that they were enough. I would have told them they are not dealing with an identity crisis because our identity is in

Christ. I would have searched our family and worked to bring us to an understanding that we are enough! I would have taken more risks instead of skirting the edge of the pool wall, limiting my thoughts, behaviors, dreams, and abilities. Without the fear of betrayal, abandonment, or rejection, I would have been more trusting. The "Goliath" of my life would have been defeated. I would not have kept God at arms' length and would have been able to dream greater dreams instead of focusing on what I thought wrong with me.

Had I known who I was, I would have lived in the "now" and not in fear of what might happen. I would not have lived for the "gonna,"…the time when I thought everything would work out, when I would be fixed. In addition, I would have listened to and trusted the Lord by embracing His love for me instead of fighting Him and contradicting what He said about me. Knowing what I know now, I would have done things differently. I would have embraced all of myself, and helped others see the love God has for them. I would have recognized my value and shown others that their true value rests in the Creator, God! The person who God created me to be has existed since the beginning. It is not a place, thing or something I ascribe to be…but God's creation is who I am *now*.

Confronting family patterns and discovering information about my family included more than stories and words on a page. It required me to take a hard look at my perception and how these pieces contributed to "who" I thought I was. I cannot blame others for the plights in my life; I am responsible. Researching for information was only the first part of the journey to knowing my "who;" however, I was not prepared for the emotional tension part of the journey.

Patterns

The emotional tension forced me to review past family dynamics dealing with marginalization, religious beliefs, racism, and poverty. I knew nothing about patterns in my life until one day, I remember struggling through a situation and suddenly remembering I had lived this before. It was here I discovered patterns. Before discovering patterns, I attributed my experiences to my immaturity or lack of understanding of my life situations, so I just lived to "do." A situation presented itself and I tried to figure out how to fix it. After many years in the church, I knew something was wrong, but didn't know what. I also did not know that patterns repeated in families. Even if I did know, I had little information about my family to put those pieces together.

At first, I was excited to learn more about my family. However, the excitement turned to anger, rage, and bitterness as I learned the history surrounding them and myself. The secrets they kept were an almost disregard for what my brothers and I endured. These secrets were between family members that began to unfold after they died. Despite confronting my mother with questions about what she allowed to happen to us; little else was said on the matter. I wanted to talk about everything and I asked questions if daddy was my father and was she my mother? The lack of the truth about my family resulted in my being consumed with negative emotions towards my parents and family members. I wanted them to feel the pain my brothers and I went through.

I discovered that feelings are living and breathing things experienced uniquely by the individual. No one can tell you how to feel or give you permission not to feel a certain way. When I learned that my dad was saved, I really got upset with God. I thought, "How can you forgive him after what he did to us?" I was so upset when his other children spoke of a loving, caring, parent who took care of and loved them when all we had were the labels of our youth from the same father they loved that did not give us his name or his presence. I hated the actions that affected my brothers and me. I heard so many messages to get over it, move beyond it, and forgive. But I did not know what *getting over it meant* or how to move beyond what you do not know?

Despite the limited information, I found family abuse, betrayal, abandonment, and rejection patterns. In addition, I found family members with similar gifts and talents in drawing and painting, music, and crafting. I had no idea that the secret to knowing "who" I was would be found in learning the past. Moreover, I did not comprehend my past impact on the present. I also faced an unexpected dilemma of forgiveness. After all, forgiveness was the furthest thing from my mind when I started the journey to discover my family. I found that forgiveness was a process that did not happen overnight. An unexpected blessing amid this journey was that I found forgiveness for myself as I worked through forgiving those for their roles in my life.

As I write *Skirting*, I find it easier to recognize when I am walking in "do"ing or walking in "who"ing. The pathway from "do" to "who" required endurance, being still, and surrendering my way of "do"ing to the Lord. I recognize His love for me because I am His and I belong to Him. Even when I mess up, sin, or ignore Him, I am no less the daughter of the Most High God. I now know God's love was never established in my "do" or my perception of myself, because He *is* love.

Reflecting on

The pathway to finding my "who" was not easy; however, I found it rewarding. I had to recognize something was going on, patterns that kept emerging despite my efforts to fix them. Although I did not know what was going on in my life, I soon learned the same patterns existed before I knew they did. Upon facing another "Goliath," I finally surrendered to God! I wanted a quick fix; after all, God is the God of everything and He surely can grant me a quick miracle, right? No, that is not right. It took years of struggling and making my way and it was going to take time, effort, surrender, and determination. God begins at the root (what is not seen), but I was going for the fruit (what I could see). I wanted Him to "fix" what I thought was going on so I could have what He promised. However, I had to go back to my past to find out "who" I was for that to happen.

God wants us to know "who" we are more than we do. "Who" you are, bears in mind what has happened to you, but does not base "who" you are on what has happened to you. Before anything ever happened to you, God already loved, approved, and had a good plan for you. What happened to you in life never changed God's mind or His plan. It is important that we realize the plan and purpose for our lives is His. Everything we "do" comes from "who" we are in Him when we walk in "who" we are.

I had to commit to doing the work necessary to learn "who" I am. Sometimes I faced long forgotten memories of trauma, abuse, and fear along the path to finding my "who." Often, discovery may require time to process what is learned; other times, discovery may bring a sigh of relief, much like finding a precious piece of you. To those on a journey to discovery I want to caution you not to take the journey lightly or without counting up the cost emotionally and physically. I urge you to invite the Lord *first*...taking the Lord, a trusted friend or family member, or even a therapist because some people, places, and situations, maybe dangerous, emotionally and physically. There are many ways to search using online resources: the Census, one of the DNA sites, a local library, friends, or family.

I experienced emotional highs and lows; searching, asking, and listening. I also wrestled with my belief in God, if He loved me, why was my life such a mess, why was life not better for me and why someone did not come to rescue my family? I questioned His justice, His goodness, and His love. But I found that Jesus Christ is the vindicator and no one is above Him. He intervened in my family member's lives but remember, people had a choice to listen or ignore Him.

The patterns in our lives are there for a reason and should not be ignored. We must pay close attention to the patterns and prayerfully take them to the Lord to find out why they are there and how to resolve them. The patterns are not there to condemn you, break you, or for you to carry that unbearable burden. I did not know patterns existed but knew things in my life were repeatedly occurring. The patterns are there for you to learn "who" you are, to discover you were never a mistake, and your life is not at the mercy of what happened to you. When I recognized myself skirting the edge of the pool wall, I did not know what it meant, but I knew I had to know why. I did not know that the answers lie within me, my history, what I believed about myself, and ultimately, what I believed about God.

Finally, when I began this journey, I wanted to fix myself. I had no idea healing was what I needed; healing from trauma, abuse, disappointments, and loss of identity. Healing from my belief that God was an uncaring Father, healing from my idea that I was never going to be enough, and from the belief that I was cursed. I lived under a shadow of shame, brokenness, and not being enough. But thanks be to God who gives us the victory through Jesus Christ our Lord (1 Corinthians 15:57 KJV), I am enough! The healing process had already been provided for me before the foundation of the world and it was found in Jesus Christ alone.

I thought finding "who" would fix circumstances in my life, but I am so grateful the process of finding my "who" brought much more… healing I did not know I needed… healing from the past experiences that haunted me…healing from the loss of identity through misuse and abuse. I am healed from the lack of belongingness because I know "who" I am and whose I am…I am joined to Jesus Christ, the one who loves me, only has good plans for me, and gave Himself a ransom for me. Knowing "who" I am has brought me peace. I am now able to "do," not because of what somebody said or did not say, but because of what Jesus Christ said. Hence "do"ing is anchored in Him! Because HE is…I "do" this or that, and because HE is my foundation, I teach, and because I am His, I live out my "who."

Conclusion

"Do"ing is forever rooted in circumstances, experiences, and fear and will never lead to your "who." According to Lindsey (2014), you will not stumble your way into purpose, since purpose emanates from identity. But "do"ing rooted in "who" you have no limitations. The only way to learn "who" you are is to go to God, our creator. Please do not allow your past to keep you in a perpetual "do"ing pattern. No matter how much you "do," you cannot satisfy your longings, silence the voices of inadequacies you hear, or heal the broken places in your life. That is why your "do" alone will never guide you to your purpose or lead you to "who" you are.

Are you a "do"-er or a "who"-er?

Alternatively, I recognize that many of you may not have experienced abuse or trauma in your life; however, many of you have wasted years "do"ing. Here is an invitation to recognize if you are a "do"-er or a "who"-er. Look at the following questions and see if you can identify any patterns or associations. Based on my experience of "do"ing I have generated some questions that may help you recognize patterns and behaviors that may identify you as a "do"er. Ask yourself:

☐ Am I a people pleaser or one that never feels they belong?

☐ Are you a job hopper/church hopper?

- ☐ Are you caught between two opinions all the time or trying to find your way…just cannot make up your mind?

- ☐ Are you doing what you're doing because you believe this is who you are?

- ☐ Do you think you will be nothing if you cannot do what you do anymore or who are you when you can no longer do it?

- ☐ Are you searching for identity…are you sure of who you are?

- ☐ Do you believe what has happened to you is who you are?

- ☐ When change occurs, do you struggle to try to figure out what you must have done wrong?

- ☐ Are your conversations with yourself always critical and are you bullying yourself into "do"ing better?

- ☐ Do you feel you do not belong or *not* feel connected with family, friends or relationships?

- ☐ Do you have reoccurring dreams, patterns or situations that end badly?

- ☐ Are you "do"ing because you want to have worth or want to feel valuable?

- ☐ Are you "do"ing based on who you or others *think* you are?

Earlier, I stated there is no amount of "do"ing you can do to satisfy your longings or silence the voices of inadequacies you hear. That's why "do" cannot guide you to purpose. My "do" kept my focus on my ability. The single-minded focus of "do" ignores who you are and draws attention to who you are not. "Do" does not live in the moment with gratitude but believes that you will have something to be grateful for once you "do" enough.

I spent years trying to make myself valuable. Even after accepting Jesus Christ as my Savior, I believed I had to prove my value to Him and others. I also believed it was up to me to protect myself. I believed I alone would figure out what I needed to do to fix myself. I listened to other voices I believed were greater, smarter, and wiser than mine, even when the words contradicted what I knew.

Moreover, I listened and followed ideas that seemed to make sense to me. I read, understood, and believed the Bible based on my distorted understanding that was rooted in my past. The "do"ing without knowing my "who" kept me skirting the edge of the pool wall. I was sure the only way to fix myself was by creating another "do" strategy that would ultimately increase my value.

I now know that finding my "who" meant discovering that I was already loved for who I was. I learned love was not because of the great or small things I had done. I understood I was looking for love, acceptance, and value in what I could "do." I was lost in the past I did not know. But God already knew me, had found me, loved me, and guided me through the good, the bad, the ugly, and the confusion. He also picked up all of the broken pieces of my life and put them back where they should have been. For only He knew each piece of my puzzle…He did not frown at it, nor distance Himself from it, He loves me right in the middle of it all.

Holding God's hand gave me the courage I never knew I had. Knowing He knows every part of me and demonstrated to me the God I never really knew. Most importantly, finding my "who" helped me to realize I was not at the mercy of my circumstances even when I believed I was. Ultimately I discovered I always had a choice. I could either reach out to God, or remain skirted to the edge of the pool wall, lost in the wilderness of my ancestors' past. I found courage, forgiveness, and freedom along this journey. I also recognize I do not need anyone's permission to be "who" I am.

References

65 Different Skirt Styles (Mega Skirt Chart). (2021). Retrieved from, January 3, 2018, from https://threadcurve.com/types-of-skirts/

Jacobs, M. (2021). What Are Pleats? A Comprehensive Guide to Different Pleat Types and How to Wear Pleats. Retrieved from, https://www.masterclass.com/articles/what-are-pleats-a-comprehensive-guide-to-different-pleat-types-and-how-to-wear-pleats

Lindsey, C. (2014). Conversations with Cornelius Ep9 "Purpose and Identity." Retrieved from, https://www.youtube.com/watch?v=7CDtkMlYq_0

Merriam-Webster. (n.d.). Skirt. In *Merriam-Webster.com dictionary*. Retrieved February 7, 2022, from https://www.merriam-webster.com/dictionary/skirt

Retrieved October 17, 2021, from https://www.merriam-webster.com/dictionary/skirt

Tortter, L. (1919). Parables of the Cross. Retrieved February 14, 2022, from https://libquotes.com/lilias-trotter/works/parables-of-the-cross

Vidor, King, Victor Fleming, George Cukor, Richard Thorpe, Norman Taurog, and Mervyn LeRoy. 1939. The Wizard of Oz. United States: Metro-Goldwyn-Mayer (MGM).

Author's Words and Definitions

The following terms are my definitions unique to this book and ascribed meaning by the author.

"Do" or "do"ing-is the action necessary to accomplish something. "Do"ing is neither good nor bad; however, it requires a reason or motivation. "Do"ing is based on one's effort and often rooted in experiences or circumstances.

"Do"-er- is an individual who equates their identity with what they have done or has been done to them. The do-er does to be or identify with (role, title, beliefs, trophies, and labels) and believes "who" they are, is what they "do."

Skirter-a person that intentionally or unintentionally chooses to not take risks in an effort to protect themselves; a person held hostage by their known or unknown past.

Skirting-is the feeling of being stuck often associated with fear, resulting in an inability to move forward.

"Who," "who" I am- is the identity God assigned to me. "Who" is neither based on one's efforts or circumstances nor one's past or present. "Who" originates with the Lord and is the complete person He created us to be.

"Who"-er-is one walking in the knowledge of their God given identity and purpose.

www.ingramcontent.com/pod-product-compliance
Ingram Content Group UK Ltd.
Pitfield, Milton Keynes, MK11 3LW, UK
UKHW022220230426
12048UKWH00016BA/962